RANDY'S CORNER

DAY BY DAY WITH...

JENNIFER LOPEZ

BY
TAMMY GAGNE

Mitchell Lane
PUBLISHERS
P.O. Box 196
Hockessin, Delaware 19707
Visit us on the web: www.mitchelllane.com

Mitchell Lane
PUBLISHERS

Printing   1   2   3   4   5   6   7   8   9

RANDY'S CORNER

DAY BY DAY WITH. . .

Adam Jones	Justin Bieber
Alex Morgan	LeBron James
Beyoncé	Manny Machado
Bindi Sue Irwin	Mia Hamm
Calvin Johnson	Miley Cyrus
Carrie Underwood	Missy Franklin
Chloë Moretz	Selena Gomez
Dwayne "The Rock" Johnson	Serena Williams
Elena Delle Donne	Shakira
Eli Manning	Shaun White
Gabby Douglas	Stephen Hillenburg
Jennifer Lopez	Taylor Swift
	Willow Smith

Library of Congress Cataloging-in-Publication Data
Gagne, Tammy.
 Day by day with Jennifer Lopez / by Tammy Gagne.
    pages cm. — (Randy's corner)
 Includes bibliographical references and index.
 ISBN 978-1-68020-113-0 (library bound)
1. Lopez, Jennifer, 1970- —Juvenile literature. 2. Actors—United States—Biography—Juvenile literature. 3. Singers—United States—Biography—Juvenile literature. 4. Hispanic American actors—Biography—Juvenile literature. 5. Hispanic American singers—Biography—Juvenile literature. I. Title.
 PN2287.L634G35 2015
 791.4302′8092—dc23
 [B]
                                                                    2015017389
eBook ISBN: 978-1-68020-114-7

ABOUT THE AUTHOR: Tammy Gagne has written dozens of books for children, including *Ariana Grande* and *Shakira* for Mitchell Lane Publishers. She resides in northern New England with her husband and son. One of her favorite pastimes is visiting schools to speak to kids about the writing process.

PUBLISHER'S NOTE: The following story has been thoroughly researched and to the best of our knowledge represents a true story. While every possible effort has been made to ensure accuracy, the publisher will not assume liability for damages caused by inaccuracies in the data and makes no warranty on the accuracy of the information contained herein. This story has not been authorized or endorsed by Jennifer Lopez.

DAY BY DAY WITH **JENNIFER LOPEZ**

You may know her as the female judge from *American Idol.* You may also be a fan of the many songs she has recorded. You might have even seen her in movies like *The Wedding Planner* or *Maid in Manhattan.* No matter where you have seen Jennifer Lopez, though, you almost certainly know who she is.

STEVEN TYLER

4

RANDY
JACKSON

5

JENNIFER LOPEZ ON STAGE WITH MARC ANTHONY AT THE 53RD ANNUAL GRAMMY AWARDS

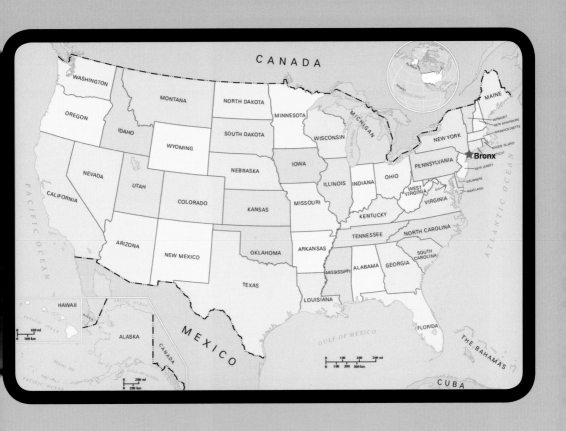

Today J-Lo, as she is sometimes called, seems to be everywhere. She even has her own lines of clothing and perfumes. She has won American Music awards, Grammys, and even Teen Choice awards. But not so long ago, she was just a girl growing up in the Bronx in New York City.

SISTERS LESLIE AND LYNDA WITH THEIR MOTHER AND GRANDMOTHER

On July 24, 1969, David and Guadalupe Lopez welcomed their second daughter, Jennifer Lynn. In an interview with *W* magazine, Jennifer shared, "I'm the middle sister. All three of us girls shared a room. I was into sports and dancing. I ran track. I have a lot of stamina. I was built for the long run."

JENNIFER LOPEZ WITH DAVID AND GUADALUPE LOPEZ AND FAMILY

JENNIFER LOPEZ PERFORMS FOR HER FANS.

And a long run it has been. After studying ballet in high school, Lopez decided to pursue a full-time dancing career. She moved out when she was 18. "A few months later," she told *W*, "I landed a job dancing in Europe. When I got back, I [got a part in] *In Living Color*. I became a Fly Girl and moved to [Los Angeles, CA]. It all happened in a year." The hit Fox television show proved to be her big break.

Jennifer also landed jobs dancing in music videos. In 1993 she appeared in Janet Jackson's video for "That's the Way Love Goes." Soon she made the jump from music to movies. She co-starred in the action flick *Money Train* in 1995 and the comedy *Jack* in 1996. But the role that would change her life was that of Selena in the 1997 film of the same name.

JENNIFER PERFORMS IN
THE MOVIE *SELENA*

JENNIFER AND SELENA'S
FAMILY REACT AFTER
JENNIFER PERFORMS A
TRIBUTE TO SELENA.

More than 11,000 young women showed up to try out for the role of the young Tejano (Mexican or Spanish from Texas) singer who was murdered by her fan club manager. Jennifer resembles the image of Selena.

Although Jennifer is also a talented singer, Selena's family, who were closely involved in the film, asked her to lip sync to Selena's original recordings. The film was an instant success.

Jennifer was becoming known as a triple threat. This entertainment term means a person who can act, dance, and sing. Just when things couldn't look any brighter for the rising star, she added the new job of

model to her résumé. Executives at the cosmetic company L'Oreal noticed how beautiful Jennifer looked at the Academy Awards. She signed a contract to appear in their ads.

JENNIFER LOPEZ PERFORMING AT THE IHEARTRADIO ULTIMATE POOL PARTY IN MIAMI BEACH, FLORIDA

18

When Sony Records offered Jennifer the opportunity to make a music album, she jumped at the chance. She released *On the 6* in 1999. The title referred to the train she used to ride to her dance lessons in the Bronx. The album produced five hit singles. No one would be asking her to lip sync again.

JENNIFER LOPEZ SINGS ON STAGE WITH MARC ANTHONY AT THE 32ND ANNIVERSARY CAROUSEL OF HOPE GALA IN BEVERLY HILLS, CALIFORNIA.

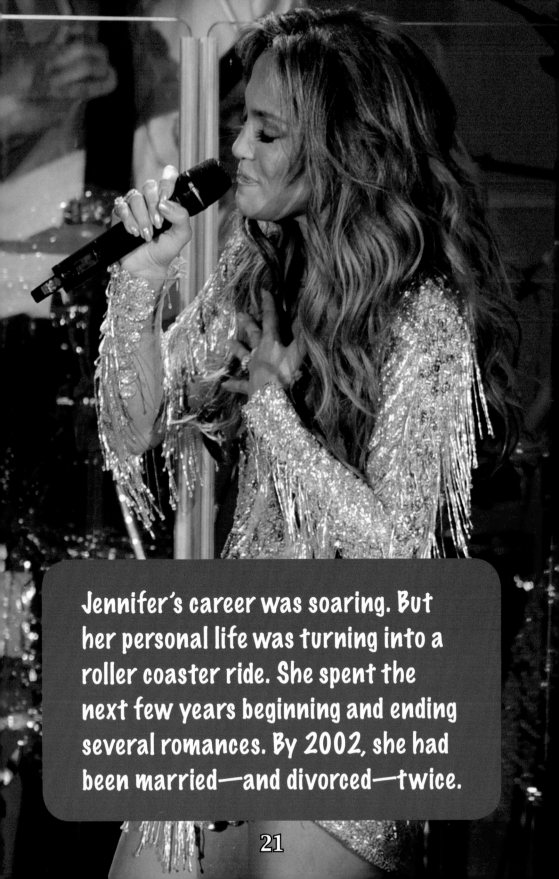

Jennifer's career was soaring. But her personal life was turning into a roller coaster ride. She spent the next few years beginning and ending several romances. By 2002, she had been married—and divorced—twice.

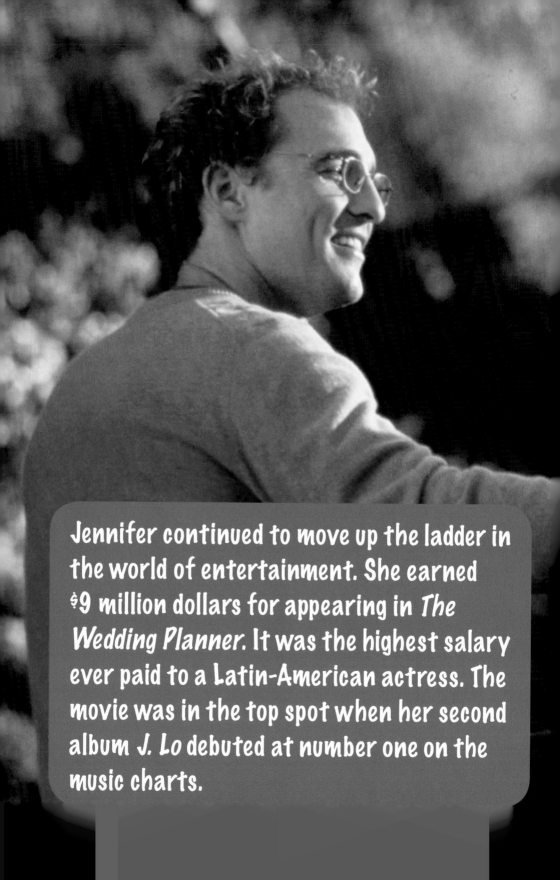

Jennifer continued to move up the ladder in the world of entertainment. She earned $9 million dollars for appearing in *The Wedding Planner*. It was the highest salary ever paid to a Latin-American actress. The movie was in the top spot when her second album *J. Lo* debuted at number one on the music charts.

JENNIFER LOPEZ ACTING WITH MATTHEW MCCONAUGHEY IN THE 2001 MOVIE *THE WEDDING PLANNER*

In 2004, Jennifer married musician Marc Anthony in Beverly Hills. The couple spent the next few years developing their careers, both together and separately. In 2008, they welcomed not just one, but two children. Jennifer gave birth to twins Emme and Max in February.

Although Jennifer and Marc divorced in 2011, their family has remained a top priority. They share custody of the twins and get along well. "Marc and I are very good friends, we're very supportive," she told the *Huffington Post*. When one parent has to work, the other cares for the children.

Work keeps Jennifer busy. In addition to her acting and music, she now hosts *American Idol*. She is also executive producer of the ABC Family hit television show *The Fosters*.

But she still finds time to help others. Her Lopez Family Foundation provides health care for families who cannot afford it.

JENNIFER WAS EXCITED TO RECEIVE THE ICON AWARD AT THE 2014 BILLBOARD MUSIC AWARDS.

What Jennifer will do next is anyone's guess. But whatever it is, she is sure to succeed. Even after so many of her dreams have come true, she continues to think about the next step. As she told *W* magazine, "I've always had dreams—the dreams have just gotten bigger."

FURTHER READING

FIND OUT MORE

Gibson, Karen Bush. *Jennifer Lopez*. Hockessin, DE: Mitchell Lane Publishers, 2011.

Lopez Family Foundation http://www.lopezfamilyfoundation.org/

Shoup, Kate. *Jennifer Lopez*. New York: Cavendish Square Publishing, 2015.

Tieck, Sarah. *Jennifer Lopez*. Edina, MA: Big Buddy Books, 2012.

WORKS CONSULTED

Fowler, Maria. "J. Lo on 'American Idol,' Madonna and her 40s.'" *USA Today*. November 6, 2014. http://www.usatoday.com/story/life/people/2014/11/06/jennifer-lopez-interview/18592785/

Hirschberg, Lynn. "Jennifer Lopez: Dream Girl." *W*. July 9, 2013. http://www.wmagazine.com/people/celebrities/2013/07/jennifer-lopez-august-2013-cover/

Hiscock, John. "Jennifer Lopez tells how her beloved children are her priority and why she's happy to be single after three husbands." *Daily Record*. October 16, 2014. http://www.dailyrecord.co.uk/entertainment/celebrity-interviews/jennifer-lopez-tells-how-beloved-4445794

_____. "Jennifer Lopez." *People.com*. http://www.people.com/people/jennifer_lopez/biography/

Reich, Ashley. "Jennifer Lopez Talks Co-Parenting with Ex Marc Anthony: He and I Are 'Very Good Friends.'" *Huffington Post*. November 4, 2014. http://www.huffingtonpost.com/2014/11/04/jennifer-lopez-marc-anthony-coparent_n_6101718.html

INDEX